# Holiday Fun

Katie Peters

GRL Consultant Diane Craig,
Certified Literacy Specialist

Lerner Publications ◆ Minneapolis

## Note from a GRL Consultant
This Pull Ahead leveled book has been carefully designed for beginning readers. A team of guided reading literacy experts has reviewed and leveled the book to ensure readers pull ahead and experience success.

Lerner Publications
An imprint of Lerner Publishing Group, Inc.
241 First Avenue North
Minneapolis, MN 55401 USA

For reading levels and more information, look up this title at www.lernerbooks.com.

Main body text set in Memphis Pro 24/39
Typeface provided by Linotype.

Photo Acknowledgments
The images in this book are used with the permission of: © domin_domin/iStockphoto, p. 3; © kali9/iStockphoto, pp. 4–5; © monkeybusinessimages/iStockphoto, pp. 6–7, 16 (turkey); © PeopleImages/iStockphoto, pp. 8–9, 16 (card); © Imgorthand/iStockphoto, pp. 10–11, 16 (guitar); © Sean Locke Photography/Shutterstock Images, pp. 12–13; © SDI Productions/iStockphoto, pp. 14–15.

Front cover: © kali9/iStockphoto

## Library of Congress Cataloging-in-Publication Data

Names: Peters, Katie, author.
Title: Holiday fun / Katie Peters ; GRL Consultant Diane Craig, Certified Literacy Specialist.
Description: Minneapolis, MN : Lerner Publications, [2023] | Audience: Ages 4–7 | Audience: Grades K–1 | Summary: "Emergent readers will delight with parts of holiday celebrations. This title features carefully leveled nonfiction text. Pairs with the fiction book, Kwanzaa Candles"— Provided by publisher.
Identifiers: LCCN 2022006207 (print) | LCCN 2022006208 (ebook) | ISBN 9781728475967 (library binding) | ISBN 9781728478883 (paperback) | ISBN 9781728483788 (ebook)
Subjects: LCSH: Holidays—Juvenile literature.
Classification: LCC GT3933 .P46 2023 (print) | LCC GT3933 (ebook) | DDC 394.26—dc23

LC record available at https://lccn.loc.gov/2022006207
LC ebook record available at https://lccn.loc.gov/2022006208

Manufactured in the United States of America
1 – CG – 12/15/22

# Table of Contents

# Holiday Fun

We like holidays.

We have holiday food.

We have holiday cards.

We have holiday music.

We have holiday games.

We have fun holidays!

# What holidays do you celebrate?

## Did You See It?

card

guitar

turkey

## Index